THE ARIZONA BORDER SURVEILLANCE TECHNOLOGY PLAN AND ITS IMPACT ON BORDER SECURITY

HEARING

BEFORE THE

SUBCOMMITTEE ON BORDER AND MARITIME SECURITY

OF THE

COMMITTEE ON HOMELAND SECURITY HOUSE OF REPRESENTATIVES

ONE HUNDRED THIRTEENTH CONGRESS

SECOND SESSION

MARCH 12, 2014

Serial No. 113–55

Printed for the use of the Committee on Homeland Security

Available via the World Wide Web: http://www.gpo.gov/fdsys/

U.S. GOVERNMENT PRINTING OFFICE

88–172 PDF   WASHINGTON : 2014

For sale by the Superintendent of Documents, U.S. Government Printing Office
Internet: bookstore.gpo.gov   Phone: toll free (866) 512–1800; DC area (202) 512–1800
Fax: (202) 512–2250   Mail: Stop SSOP, Washington, DC 20402–0001

COMMITTEE ON HOMELAND SECURITY

MICHAEL T. MCCAUL, Texas, *Chairman*

LAMAR SMITH, Texas
PETER T. KING, New York
MIKE ROGERS, Alabama
PAUL C. BROUN, Georgia
CANDICE S. MILLER, Michigan, *Vice Chair*
PATRICK MEEHAN, Pennsylvania
JEFF DUNCAN, South Carolina
TOM MARINO, Pennsylvania
JASON CHAFFETZ, Utah
STEVEN M. PALAZZO, Mississippi
LOU BARLETTA, Pennsylvania
RICHARD HUDSON, North Carolina
STEVE DAINES, Montana
SUSAN W. BROOKS, Indiana
SCOTT PERRY, Pennsylvania
MARK SANFORD, South Carolina
VACANCY

BENNIE G. THOMPSON, Mississippi
LORETTA SANCHEZ, California
SHEILA JACKSON LEE, Texas
YVETTE D. CLARKE, New York
BRIAN HIGGINS, New York
CEDRIC L. RICHMOND, Louisiana
WILLIAM R. KEATING, Massachusetts
RON BARBER, Arizona
DONDALD M. PAYNE, JR., New Jersey
BETO O'ROURKE, Texas
TULSI GABBARD, Hawaii
FILEMON VELA, Texas
STEVEN A. HORSFORD, Nevada
ERIC SWALWELL, California

VACANCY, *Staff Director*
MICHAEL GEFFROY, *Deputy Staff Director/Chief Counsel*
MICHAEL S. TWINCHEK, *Chief Clerk*
I. LANIER AVANT, *Minority Staff Director*

————

SUBCOMMITTEE ON BORDER AND MARITIME SECURITY

CANDICE S. MILLER, Michigan, *Chairwoman*

JEFF DUNCAN, South Carolina
TOM MARINO, Pennsylvania
STEVEN M. PALAZZO, Mississippi
LOU BARLETTA, Pennsylvania
VACANCY
MICHAEL T. MCCAUL, Texas *(Ex Officio)*

SHEILA JACKSON LEE, Texas
LORETTA SANCHEZ, California
BETO O'ROURKE, Texas
TULSI GABBARD, Hawaii
BENNIE G. THOMPSON, Mississippi *(Ex Officio)*

PAUL L. ANSTINE, II, *Subcommittee Staff Director*
DEBORAH JORDAN, *Subcommittee Clerk*
ALISON NORTHROP, *Minority Subcommittee Staff Director*

CONTENTS

THE ARIZONA BORDER SURVEILLANCE TECHNOLOGY PLAN AND ITS IMPACT ON BORDER SECURITY

Wednesday, March 12, 2014

U.S. HOUSE OF REPRESENTATIVES,
SUBCOMMITTEE ON BORDER AND MARITIME SECURITY,
COMMITTEE ON HOMELAND SECURITY,
Washington, DC.

The subcommittee met, pursuant to call, at 10:06 a.m., in Room 311, Cannon House Office Building, Hon. Candice S. Miller [Chairwoman of the subcommittee] presiding.

Present: Representatives Miller, Duncan, Jackson Lee, O'Rourke, and Gabbard.

Mrs. MILLER. The Committee on Homeland Security, our Subcommittee on Border and Maritime Security will come to order.

The subcommittee is meeting today to examine the CBP's border technology plan and its impact on securing our Nation's borders, and we are very pleased today to be joined by Assistant Commissioner, Mark Borkowski, again.

Welcome back to the committee.

He is from the Office of Technology Innovation and Acquisition at the U.S. Customs and Border Protection.

Rebecca Gambler, we welcome you back to the committee as well.

Rebecca is the director of homeland security and justice issues with the Governmental Accounting Office, and I will more formally introduce them after we do our opening statements.

Technology has really been an integral part of the proposed solution to secure the vast and rugged terrain of the Southwest Border for a long time, and it is one part of an overall set of solutions that must include manpower, intelligence, and where appropriate, infrastructure.

Unfortunately, a series of miscues and missteps has plagued Customs and Border Protection's previous efforts to produce a large-scale border security solution.

The prior program known as SBInet was the subject of many criticisms from the GAO and the Congress before then-Secretary Napolitano canceled the program actually in 2011, and our goal in holding today's hearing is to ensure that we are finally on the path to success after a number of false starts.

Hundreds of millions of dollars were spent for SBInet. We have a grand total of 53 miles of the border under surveillance to show for it. That is just 53 miles out of nearly 2,000, so I don't think any of us can say that that is an acceptable outcome.

I am sure there is enough blame to go around for that, but we are not here today to assign blame. We are here today to make sure that moving forward the American people get the border security that they need, that they want, that they have paid for, certainly that they deserve.

In this time of limited budgets we cannot repeat the mistakes of the past and this subcommittee will hold the CBP accountable to ensure that the largest and most expensive part of the Arizona Border Surveillance Technology Plan, the integrated fixed towers, is on track.

Years of delay have not inspired Congressional confidence in the IFT project or the larger Arizona Border Surveillance Technology Plan. According to the GAO report said to be released today, some of the smaller-scale purchases do not meet the needs of the Border Patrol and others have been contracting challenges.

More troubling, CBP did not concur with several of GAO's recommendations when it comes to testing the IFT and the integration of the smaller-scale technologies into a master schedule, and I certainly hope to hear more of the rationale for that non-concurrence.

On a very positive note, I was certainly pleased to see that the Department did release the $145 million award for the IFT contract last year—excuse me, last week—but for many of us in Congress, this is a project that has certainly taken far too long.

It has been 3 years since the cancellation of SBInet. We may not see additional border security capabilities come on-line until later this summer. To that end, we are troubled as well by the current roll-out time line that will deploy eight towers fairly rapidly in the Nogales area, but then we are going to have a gap of time before other towers are deployed.

Mr. Borkowski is shaking his head, so I know he is going to be addressing these concerns, and I appreciate that. I certainly would encourage the Department to move quickly to resolve any outstanding impediments to the deployment of this technology quickly consistent with the operational needs of the men and women of the Border Patrol.

It has taken several years to get technology deployed to Arizona and in that time the threat has shifted actually to south Texas. Our procurement process has to be more agile and quicker otherwise by the time we deploy a solution, the threat may have moved elsewhere.

I also want to work with the Office of Technology Innovation and Analysis to help bring effective technology to the border faster. We should look to the Department of Defense and some of the novel models that they have used to solve this very challenge.

Our committee and this subcommittee in particular has a vested interest in securing the border. We have worked on a bipartisan basis to pass legislation that defines operational control as a 90 percent effectiveness rate and as for a comprehensive border security technology plan so that the Department is not putting technology on the border in an ad hoc way.

Each piece of technology that we put on the border should align with the Border Patrol's operational needs and must support the twin goals of increasing our situational awareness and effectiveness in keeping those that would do us harm out of our country.

The development of border security metrics will help with this effort because without metrics there is no way to measure success or failure. Congress and the American people have to know what increase in security we are achieving with their taxpayer dollars.

GAO recommended that the Department work toward a better understanding of how technology contributes to border security and we certainly all have a very keen interest in that effort.

We certainly look forward to hearing how the Department has learned the lessons from previous failures and assurances that the taxpayers are getting tangible, measurable border security from the Arizona Border Surveillance Technology Plan.

At this time, the Chairwoman would recognize our Ranking Member of the subcommittee, the gentlelady from Texas, Ms. Jackson Lee, for any statements she may have.

Ms. JACKSON LEE. Madam Chairwoman, thank you so very much, and together we are concerned about this technology as we have been discussing technology throughout this session of Congress.

I want to acknowledge the gentleman from Texas, Mr. O'Rourke, and the gentlelady from Hawaii, Ms. Gabbard, present for this hearing. I want to thank Chairwoman Miller for holding today's hearing on the Arizona Border Surveillance Technology Plan.

As a senior Member of both this committee and the Judiciary Committee and as a Member from a border State, I have closely followed DHS' efforts to deploy much-needed technology and resources to our Southwest Border.

Unfortunately, DHS has a poor track record with its major border security technology acquisitions.

More recently, the SBInet program was canceled by Secretary Janet Neapolitan in 2011 after delivering only 53 miles of border security technology in Arizona at a cost to the American people of about $1 billion.

That is a mouthful, and I hope however that that does not alter or dismiss the value of technology and the reality that technology can really work.

Now 3 years later, CBP is moving forward with the Arizona Border Surveillance Technology Plan which is intended to provide additional border security capability in Arizona. I would take note of Congressman Barber and former Congresswoman Giffords who raised this issue continuously so I know the concept is important.

Already though, there may be some cause for concern. The Government Accountability Office released a report today that CBP is not following all best practices and DHS guidance for acquisition management with this new program.

Given the challenging nature of these kinds of acquisitions and the limited staffing resources CBP has to carry them out, it is imperative that the agency follows all guidelines to minimize risks to the plan and get a successful result.

I hope to hear in detail from our GAO witness today about what the most pressing challenges are with respect to scheduling, cost estimates, testing, and performance metrics for the plan.

I also hope our CBP witness will provide convincing answers about how they are addressing these challenges to prevent a repeat of the problems that ultimately undermine SBInet.

We simply cannot afford to spend another $1 billion on border security technology that fails to deliver as promised.

Madam Chairwoman, as I even say that amount I get a sense of fear for going down that route again. Certainly, the Border Patrol must have resources that will meet its needs to address the ever-changing threats it faces among our borders and as well those threats that impact the American people.

With that in mind, I am particularly interested in hearing from CBP about how it intends to ensure the plan technology will meet the Border Patrol's needs especially given scheduling delays that have occurred and the dynamic in nature of the border security mission.

I believe collectively Chairwoman Miller and myself have been a very supportive team of CBP. We have worked to ensure funding and I would hope that this hearing would not be perceived as accusations against CBP but only instructive collaborative efforts to make what we all want and that is a safer homeland.

Specifically it is my understanding, the chief of the Border Patrol recently communicated that his agency no longer needs as many integrated fixed towers in Arizona and instead requires more mobile technology to deploy to increasingly problematic tech areas along the border in South Texas.

Having been to the border, both borders, but in South Texas particularly at night when we first began to give mobile equipment to CBP I can assure you that it is a reality of how important that equipment is.

I hope that the needs of the Border Patrol and the requirements of their mission are always being considered throughout this process, and I look forward to hearing from our CBP witness about how this recent request will be resolved.

Again, I thank the witnesses for joining us today, and I look forward to a robust discussion about how we can ensure the Arizona border technology plan succeeds where its predecessors did not.

Madam Chairwoman, just a moment as I conclude.

All of us have had our eyes poised, if you will, on the Malaysian air liner tragically lost; our sympathy to those families who are both mourning and waiting and now in a very confused state.

But I know that everyone was struck by the issue of the false passports that two individuals managed to get on. We have no conclusion. We have speculation. We do not know.

But I know that, Madam Chairwoman, all of us on Homeland Security were aghast that most countries are not using the database check, and I believe that because we are a border security subcommittee that it would it be very helpful for us to leap into that.

I know that there is jurisdiction, cross-jurisdiction with Judiciary, but I would love to request a hearing on that because it is brought to our attention. A tragedy has occurred. We cannot suggest or we do not have the facts as to what might have provoked that, but I believe that that is a sore that is waiting to spread and creating a devastating degree of nonsecurity around the world, so

I hope that we will have a discussion about that and as we do many other items of importance.

With that, Madam Chairwoman, I yield back.

Mrs. MILLER. I thank the gentlelady. I certainly thank the gentlelady for her comments about the Malaysia flight, and as you mentioned, we all share shock and certainly our prayers going out to the families of those that are missing, where no one knows where they are or what has happened.

Certainly that is one of the great mysteries I think that any of us have ever seen, but it is interesting you mention about the passports because we have already been talking to staff about putting together sort-of looking at what is the entire passport issue and the other countries and how they are in compliance or noncompliance with looking at some of these things.

Now it appears—again speculation—we are only talking about what we are reading in the papers I guess, that these two with the stolen passports were not on the watch list, but we will see where that goes, but I certainly appreciate those comments and we do, as I think this committee, subcommittee, and our full committee needs to take a look at that entire issue as well.

In regards to the subject at hand, I would also just remind other Members of the committee that opening statements might be submitted for the record and we are certainly pleased to have as I mentioned two very distinguished witnesses to speak to our subcommittee today.

Mr. Mark Borkowski became the assistant commissioner for the Office of Technology Innovation and Acquisition at the United States Custom and Border Protection in July 2010.

In this role he is responsible for ensuring technology efforts are properly focused, on mission, and well-integrated across CBP. Prior to his appointment as assistant commissioner, Mr. Borkowski was the executive director for the Secure Border Initiative.

Ms. Rebecca Gambler—I welcome back again to the committee— is an acting director in the U.S. Government Accountability's Office of Homeland Security and Justice team. She leads GAO's work on the border security and immigration issues, and their full written statements will appear in the record.

At this point, the Chairwoman now recognizes Mr. Borkowski for his testimony.

STATEMENT OF MARK BORKOWSKI, ASSISTANT COMMISSIONER, OFFICE OF TECHNOLOGY INNOVATION AND ACQUISITION, CUSTOMS AND BORDER PROTECTION, U.S. DEPARTMENT OF HOMELAND SECURITY

Mr. BORKOWSKI. Well, thank you.

Chairwoman Miller, Ranking Member Jackson Lee, Members of the committee, thank you very much for the opportunity to come and describe to you where we have been, where we are, where we think we are going.

You laid an agenda quite a bit of material that I will do my best to cover at least with some introductory things, and I will look forward to the questions.

I also do want to note that we certainly have appreciated the support of this committee. We recognize that it has required a tremendous amount of tolerance and forbearance on your part as we have gone through the last 2 to 3 years of trying to get ourselves to the point where we finally have contracts awarded, so we appreciate the support.

We understand it has been frustrating. We understand that you are at least as frustrated as we have been by the delays, but I will try to take you through where we are, how we got there, and why we think maybe we are about to turn the corner.

You both mentioned SBInet and the history of SBInet. SBInet taught us a lot of things as we all well know. It taught us how not to buy things for the Department of Homeland Security, but as Ms. Jackson Lee mentioned, it also taught us that technology does some very good things.

Where we did deploy the two SBInet deployments, it had a near-immediate effect on our ability to deal with those areas of the border, and although I couldn't give you something more quantitative than this, as we fly over those areas today, a year or 2 years after they have been deployed, the activity in those areas is down tremendously.

So technology not only supports the actual gaining of control of an area but it tends to stand as a sentry afterwards and maintain that reduced activity which then gives us more flexibility to move Border Patrol agents and other technology, so we have learned that technology is a significant factor when it is deployed properly. So we all share the interest in getting the technology out there.

But some of the lessons that we learned from SBInet are lessons that we tried to apply into the current Arizona technology plan and there are a couple of key lessons that I want to really emphasize because they get to the point as to why we non-concurred with a couple of the GAO recommendations.

Put simply, in our view, the GAO recommendations are driving us back to what we don't want to do, an SBInet. Put simply, that is the issue.

What do I mean by that? SBInet was a system development. Now that is a term of art in my business and I have struggled with—because to me the difference between SBInet and IFT is so clear because I have done this—I have trouble explaining it—but think of it this way.

If you went to buy a car you would have a choice. You could say, "I am going to pretend there are no cars to buy, and I am just going to go ask somebody to build me a car from scratch," or you could go to a car dealer and pick what is off the lot.

We normally buy things in the Government unfortunately that first way as if there is nothing on the lot, and you can imagine what the costs, but it turns out in this business there is a lot of stuff on the lot and so we went to buy it on the lot. That is a big deal and we disaggregated pieces. We didn't tie it all together. We broke them apart.

It turns out that that has had a significant effect because in almost everything we have bought we have bought it for lower than we anticipated cost. I attribute it to the non-developmental nature and the fact that we are willing to be flexible about the technical definition of requirements and I would be prepared to discuss that in more detail as we go, to the point where we have the freed-up resources that have allowed us to do things like fly Aero stats over South Texas.

When you talk about putting things in Texas we have started to do that with money that was freed up from savings generated by the strategy in the Arizona technology development plan.

So we think we are making progress. As you mentioned, we awarded the IFT contract last week. I will tell you compared to the initial estimate, we saved 75 percent, and I know that sounds unbelievable and we are going to study that as to how did that happen.

How could it be 75 percent savings, but as we have started to dig in, we think we are learning some lessons that may apply and provide that kind of experience in the future if we change our strategies.

So in that context, as we have been buying these things, we have also been trying to strengthen our competency, the technical detail about how you buy these things and that is where the GAO has come in.

While it is true that the GAO report continues to note areas of weakness, I would also point out that if you go back over the last few years I believe if you read these reports over the last few years you are going to see an improving trend.

I believe that the issues that we are finding are becoming increasingly business frankly arcane, and we really are to the point where we have to make decisions about trading off cost versus perfection.

So while we agree with the recommendations generally, where those recommendations tell us to tie things together that should be broken apart, which is what the IMS recommendation does, or tells us to build a new car rather than buying a car on the lot, which is what the test and evaluation recommendation would tend us to, we would object to those.

We think it is a better approach to take this new method of buying—let's try that for a while and then generate lessons learned from that. So that is kind of where we are at this point. I look forward to your questions, and again, I very much appreciate the committee's support and forbearance to this point.

[The prepared statement of Mr. Borkowski follows:]

PREPARED STATEMENT OF MARK BORKOWSKI

MARCH 12, 2014

Chairwoman Miller, Ranking Member Jackson Lee, and distinguished Members of the subcommittee, it is a pleasure to appear before you today to discuss the status of U.S. Customs and Border Protection's (CBP) border security technology programs in Arizona, and to reflect on the most recent Government Accountability Office (GAO) report about the management of those programs.

I appreciate the partnership and support we have received from Congress, this subcommittee, and your staff, whose commitment to the security of the American people has enabled the continued deployment of key border security technologies, even in the face of significant challenges. I am confident that our collective efforts will continue to result in a better-managed and more secure border.

This subcommittee is familiar with the outcome of CBP's SBInet program, an earlier component of the Department of Homeland Security's (DHS) Secure Border Initiative (SBI) that was designed as a comprehensive and integrated technology program to provide persistent surveillance across the northern and southern land borders of the United States, starting with the border of Mexico. The program experienced significant schedule delays and cost overruns because it did not allow necessary flexibility to adapt to differing needs in the various regions of the border. SBInet eventually delivered systems to two Areas of Responsibility in Arizona that continue to operate successfully. Nevertheless, DHS cancelled SBI on January 14, 2011, because it was too costly and the idea of one, all-encompassing program was unnecessarily complex for border technology.

Since 2011, we have learned from the issues identified in from the SBInet approach and moved away from an all-encompassing SBInet concept. Instead, DHS and CBP have approached our border technology requirements in more manageable pieces tailored to specific regions on the border. Working closely with the Border Patrol to develop requirements, we created a menu of different, sophisticated technology systems, ranging from small to large, simple to complex. For Arizona, we selected systems from the menu and tailored those technology solutions based on realistic capabilities of current technologies and the operational needs of particular areas. We then created detailed acquisition plans for each of the technologies on the menu and have been in the process of buying and deploying them for the last few years. We refer to this approach as the Arizona Technology Plan (ATP).

ATP or "the Plan" is not a program as traditionally defined within the acquisition business. Instead, it is a set of programs that, taken together, will provide what we believe is the optimal set of systems for our current operational needs. One key point is that the Plan is not a so-called "system of systems." In fact, our acquisition strategy moved intentionally away from the "system of systems" concept because we had learned from our SBInet experience that this approach was unnecessarily complex and costly.

Another change in CBP's ATP acquisition strategy based on lessons learned from SBInet, is a shift from pursuing what is known as "system development" toward a concept of leveraging "non-developmental items." Put simply, system development involves the creation of a system that does not currently exist. System development is a very disciplined and exhaustive process that requires engineering design, analysis to compare the design to requirements, comprehensive testing, and eventually deployment and operation. System development is an appropriate acquisition approach when: (1) The requirements are understood with high confidence, (2) there is limited flexibility to relax the requirements, and (3) no existing system meets the requirements. However, system development is costly, challenging, and often risky—more so when the conditions that would support system development do not exist. In the case of SBInet, we did not have a highly confident understanding of the requirements, or a solid justification for why our requirements were inflexible. Therefore, it was unclear whether existing systems would be adequate for our needs. Based on lessons learned from SBInet, we explicitly and intentionally rejected system development as our approach for the programs within the Plan.

For the programs under the ATP, we embarked on a non-developmental item (NDI) approach because after conducting extensive market research, we had high confidence that technology systems already existed that could provide most, if not all, of the capabilities we felt were required. CBP's Office of Technology Innovation and Acquisition (OTIA), which I oversee, worked collaboratively with the Border Patrol to develop the technical requirements. We also created the flexibility to trade those requirements against cost. Under this NDI strategy, we created an opportunity to do things like buy a system that met 90 percent of our interests at 50 percent of the cost, as compared to a system that might have met 100 percent of our interests but at twice the cost.

STATUS OF ARIZONA TECHNOLOGY PLAN PROGRAMS

While acquisition of the programs within the Plan is admittedly behind schedule I believe our actions have been prudent and have actually resulted in some very positive outcomes. In short, we elected to trade schedule for higher likelihood of success in the ultimate deployments of the NDI technologies and to take advantage of opportunities to reduce costs.

Using the NDI approach, most of the programs within the Plan are on contract and many have already been deployed, including: Agent Portable Surveillance Systems (APSS); Thermal Imaging Devices; Underground Sensors (UGS); and some Mobile Video Surveillance Systems (MSC). Although it is too early to declare complete success, the early indications of the ATP acquisition strategy are quite positive and, in some cases, far exceed our expectations.

For example, the most complex and costly program within the Plan is the Integrated Fixed Tower (IFT) program. This program, ostensibly, looks something like the old SBInet program. As such, it is often treated as if it were SBInet renamed. However, IFT is not SBInet. It is an NDI program, and it is a narrowly-tailored solution to select parts of the border.

Early external assessments of the program questioned whether NDI systems for IFT existed and whether CBP's program cost estimates were too low. While the specific numbers are still sensitive, I can report that we received far more proposals from industry for the IFT contract than we anticipated and, for that matter, more than I have ever seen for this type of procurement during my roughly 30 years in this business. The proposals were quite credible, and the sheer number rebuts any doubts about NDI availability. Also, almost every program in the Plan has been contracted at less than our initial estimates—often much less. The IFT contract, for example, came in at a savings approaching 75 percent of our initial estimate. Although we will likely have routine changes in the contract over time that will add slightly to the final cost, a 75 percent cost savings leaves a lot of room for those routine changes. It is also important to note that, because these are NDI systems, we have been able to use firm fixed-price contracting, which reduces the risk to the Government of substantial and uncontrolled cost growth, compared to cost reimbursable contracts for system developments like SBInet.

We attribute these positive indications to our acquisition strategy, our thorough market research, our staff's hard work, our willingness to trade schedule for risk reduction, and our on-going dialogue with industry. DHS and CBP acknowledged that we needed to do things differently if we wanted a better result from past acquisition failures. In a sense, our approach to the Plan was an experiment. While not without risk, we believe the plan represents the most viable option for a successful acquisition process, one that might prove to be a useful model going forward. As I indicated, we are quite encouraged by what we have seen so far.

The cost savings alone have already had a major impact for us. We have harvested those savings to do many of the things that this subcommittee has advocated. For instance, we have worked closely with the Department of Defense (DoD) to receive or borrow their technologies. We currently have three DoD aerostats flying over the Border Patrol's Rio Grande Valley Sector as part of an extended Field Deployment Evaluation. While undergoing evaluation, the systems concurrently support real-world operations and boost technological capabilities in a high-priority area of the border. We are able to fund this exercise, as well as a number of other notable efforts, because of the cost savings incurred as a result of our Arizona Technology Plan strategy.

GAO RECOMMENDATIONS

CBP's border security efforts are critically important, and we appreciate GAO's engagement with CBP's technology acquisition activities from the SBInet days through the present. GAO has been consistently objective and has always been very open to our thoughts and opinions. It is important to consider the latest GAO report in the context of our history to date. While the recent March 2014 report, "Arizona Border Surveillance Technology Plan: Additional Actions Needed to Strengthen Management and Assess Effectiveness," continues to identify some areas of potential weakness and risk, I believe it also demonstrates a continuing improvement trend. Piece by piece, we are building the program management infrastructure that did not exist in the early days of SBInet. The GAO has helped us prioritize our efforts over the years and deserves great credit for helping to point the way to better performance.

In the latest report, we concur with many of the GAO recommendations because they represent well-established best practices for any acquisition program—including the non-developmental programs that comprise the Plan. In most of these cases, we are aware of the shortcomings highlighted by the GAO. However, we also recognize that, we had to prioritize the activities that offered the least risk to our success by conducting a cost-benefit analysis. For example, although we did not complete formal independent cost estimates for our programs, we had substantial data and market research to give us high confidence in the conservatism of our life-cycle cost estimates. Similarly, while it is true that not all required acquisition documentation was formally approved at set times, the documents were virtually final, well-understood, and complete enough to enable key decisions with little risk. Going forward, we will strive to perform better in these areas.

We have non-concurred with two of the GAO recommendations, mainly because they contradict the foundation of the acquisition strategy we implemented for the Plan. Each program in the Plan has an Integrated Master Schedule (IMS), as required by our policy and practice. However, the GAO recommends CBP create an IMS for the Plan, as if the Plan itself is a program or "system of systems." As discussed above, CBP intentionally designed the Plan not to be a system of systems. It has been the separation of the old SBInet program into nearly independent and dis-aggregated elements that has, in my view, enabled the positive trends we have seen to date. We maintain an appropriate level of integration and schedule connection among the programs in the Plan; however, the GAO recommendation runs counter to the lessons learned from SBInet and risks returning us to an acquisition strategy we already know to be high-risk.

Similarly, the GAO calls for formal Operational Test and Evaluation (OT&E), as if the Plan were a system development. As noted above, CBP structured the Plan with NDI programs as a result of lessons learned from SBInet. Since we are familiar with the technologies, we are willing to trade requirements and performance for cost and other benefits. We have committed to purchasing, at firm-fixed price, a system that will perform to the specifications asserted by the contractor. Formal OT&E would create unnecessary bureaucracy, threaten the NDI nature of the program by creating a set of requirements that may demand system development activities, and compromise the nature of the Plan that has already suggested very positive results.

For example, we will manage IFT as we have done for several of the other programs in the Plan. We have worked with the Border Patrol to define the kind of operational experience and analysis Border Patrol agents believe they need to understand and assess the system performance. We have documented this agreement in the Test and Evaluation Master Plan. This meets much of the intent of formal OT&E, does it without unnecessary bureaucracy, and provides the Border Patrol with oversight, control, and data to influence decisions about future deployments and potential system upgrades.

CONCLUSION

In short, we concur with the GAO where the recommendations represent best practices and risk reduction for acquisitions like the Arizona Technology Plan. We do not concur where those recommendations are inconsistent with the intentional design of the programs in the Plan and where implementation of those recommendations would compromise the foundation of the Plan.

Some have characterized our acquisition approach to the Plan as innovative—especially with regard to how it leverages NDI opportunities and offers an opportunity to trade-off requirements. Innovation in acquisition means we will apply lessons learned, experiment with new things, and break new ground. We have a solid understanding of where we need to break new ground, and we look forward to working with the GAO as we continue our efforts to develop what could become a new set of best practices.

Chairwoman Miller, Ranking Member Jackson Lee, thank you for the opportunity to testify today. I look forward to your questions.

Mrs. MILLER. I thank the gentleman very much. I think we do have a lot of questions after that.

At this time, the Chairwoman now recognizes Ms. Gambler.

STATEMENT OF REBECCA GAMBLER, DIRECTOR, HOMELAND SECURITY AND JUSTICE ISSUES, U.S. GOVERNMENT AC-COUNTABILITY OFFICE

Ms. GAMBLER. Good morning, Chairwoman Miller, Ranking Member Jackson Lee, and Members of the subcommittee.

I appreciate the opportunity to testify in today's hearing to discuss GAO's work reviewing the status of DHS' Arizona Border Surveillance Technology Plan.

This plan followed DHS' announcement in January 2011 that it was canceling further procurements of Secure Border Initiative Network Systems referred to as SBInet. DHS announced the launch of the secure border initiative in 2005 as a multi-year, multi-billion-dollar program aimed at securing U.S. borders.

SBInet was intended to include various technologies such as fixed sensor towers and tactical infrastructure to create a virtual fence along the Southwest Border.

After a cost of about $1 billion, SBInet systems are now operating along 53 miles of Arizona's border.

The Arizona Border Surveillance Technology Plan includes a mix of radars, sensors, and cameras to provide security for the remainder of the Arizona border.

My remarks today will focus on three areas related to CBP's management of the plan and its efforts to assess the contributions of planned and deployed technologies to border security.

First, we reviewed CBP's schedules and life-cycle cost estimates for the plan and its highest-cost programs and we compared them against best practices. Those best practices, if followed consistently, are designed to help agencies better ensure the reliability of their schedules and cost estimates.

Overall, the schedules and estimates for the plan's programs reflected as some but not all best practices. For example, we found that the schedules for some of the programs were not fully credible because CBP had not identified all risks that would be most likely to delay the programs.

CBP also has not developed an integrated master schedule for the plan. Such a schedule could help provide CBP with a comprehensive view of the plan and more reliably commit to when the plan will be fully implemented.

We also found that CBP has not independently verify its life-cycle cost estimates for two of the plan's programs, the integrated fixed towers and remote video surveillance system.

Second, we reviewed the extent to which CBP followed key aspects of DHS' acquisition guidance in managing the plan. CBP followed this guidance in some areas, but for the plan's three highest cost programs we found that DHS and CBP did not consistently approve key acquisition documents when called for in DHS' guidance.

For example, for the integrated fixed towers DHS approved four of the six required documents at the time they were to be approved but two other documents, the life-cycle cost estimate and the test plan were not approved on time based on documentation we received from CBP.

With regard to the test plan this plan calls for CBP to conduct limited user testing of the integrated fixed tower to determine mission contributions for 30 days at one site along the Arizona border, however such an approach is not consistent with DHS' acquisition guidance which calls for operational tests and evaluation of systems to occur in the environmental conditions in which a system will be used.

Conducting unlimited user tests at one location for 30 days could limit the information available to CBP on how the towers will perform in other locations and under different environmental conditions along the border.

More robust testing is particularly important in light of the previous challenges we identified in testing of SBInet systems.

For example, we previously reported that some SBInet test plans were not defined in accordance with the guidance. We concluded that not doing effective testing can unnecessarily increase the risks of problems going undetected until late in a system's life cycle.

Thus, conducting more robust testing on the integrated fixed towers could help CBP better ensure that the towers meet Border Patrol's operational needs.

Finally, DHS had the database through which Border Patrol can record whether or not an asset such as a camera assisted in an apprehension or seizure. This indicator is referred to by the Border Patrol as an asset assist.

Data on asset assist, if used with other performance metrics or indicators, could help CBP assess the contributions of surveillance technologies to apprehensions and seizures. However Border Patrol does not require agents to record data on asset assist, and thus the agency does not have complete data to help assess technologies' contributions to border security efforts.

In closing, we have made recommendations to DHS in all of these areas to help the Department in its efforts to manage and implement the plan. DHS has agreed with some but not all of these recommendations and has actions planned or under way to address some of them. We will continue to monitor DHS' efforts in response to our recommendations.

This concludes my oral statement. I would be pleased to answer any questions that Members may have.

[The prepared statement of Ms. Gambler follows:]

PREPARED STATEMENT OF REBECCA GAMBLER

MARCH 12, 2014

Chairwoman Miller, Ranking Member Jackson Lee, and Members of the subcommittee: I am pleased to be here today to discuss the findings from our March 2014 report, being released today, in which we assessed the Department of Homeland Security's (DHS) U.S. Customs and Border Protection's (CBP) efforts to develop and implement the Arizona Border Surveillance Technology Plan (the Plan).[1] In recent years, nearly half of all annual apprehensions of illegal entrants along the Southwest Border with Mexico have occurred along the Arizona border, according to DHS data. A top priority for CBP is preventing, detecting, and apprehending illegal entrants. In November 2005, DHS announced the launch of the Secure Border Initiative (SBI), a multi-year, multi-billion-dollar program aimed at securing U.S. borders and reducing illegal immigration. CBP intended for the SBI Network (SBInet) to include technologies such as fixed-sensor towers, a common operating picture, and tactical infrastructure to create a "virtual fence" along the Southwest Border to enhance CBP's capability to detect, identify, classify, track, and respond to illegal breaches at and between land ports of entry.[2] At a cost of about $1 billion, in 2010, CBP deployed SBInet systems, referred to as Block 1 systems, along the 53 miles of Arizona's 387-mile border with Mexico that represent one of the highest-risk areas for illegal entry attempts. However, in January 2011, in response to internal and external assessments that dentified concerns regarding the performance, cost, and schedule for implementing the systems, the Secretary of Homeland Security announced the cancellation of further procurements of SBInet systems.[3]

After the cancellation of SBInet in January 2011, CBP developed the Plan, which includes a mix of radars, sensors, and cameras to help provide security for the remainder of the Arizona border. Under the Plan, CBP identified seven programs to be implemented ranging in estimated costs from $3 million to about $961 million. The three highest-cost programs under the Plan are the Integrated Fixed Tower

---

[1] GAO, *Arizona Border Surveillance Technology Plan: Additional Actions Needed to Strengthen Management and Assess Effectiveness*, GAO–14–368 (Washington, DC: Mar. 3, 2014).

[2] The SBInet fixed-sensor towers were intended to transmit radar and camera information into a common operating picture at work stations manned at all times by U.S. Border Patrol agents. The SBInet Common Operating Picture was intended to provide uniform data through a command center environment to Border Patrol agents in the field and all DHS agencies, and to be interoperable with the equipment of DHS external stakeholders, such as local law enforcement. Tactical infrastructure includes pedestrian and vehicle fences, roads, and lighting. Ports of entry are officially designated places that provide for the arrival at, or departure from, the United States.

[3] See, for example, GAO, *Secure Border Initiative: DHS Needs to Reconsider Its Proposed Investment in Key Technology Program*, GAO–10–340 (Washington, DC: May 5, 2010), and *Secure Border Initiative: DHS Needs to Address Significant Risks in Delivering Key Technology Investment*, GAO–08–1086 (Washington, DC: Sept. 22, 2008).

(IFT), Remote Video Surveillance System (RVSS), and Mobile Surveillance Capability (MSC), accounting for 97 percent of the Plan's estimated cost.[4] In November 2011, we reported on CBP's development of, and estimated life-cycle costs for, implementing the Plan.[5] Specifically, we reported that CBP needed more information for the Plan and its costs before proceeding with implementation, and we recommended that CBP, among other things, determine the mission benefits to be derived from the implementation of the Plan and develop and apply key attributes for metrics to assess program implementation, conduct a post implementation review and operational assessment of SBInet, and update the cost estimate for the Plan using best practices.[6] DHS concurred with these recommendations and has actions under way to address some of them.

My testimony today is based on and summarizes the key findings of our report on the status of the Plan, which was publicly released today. [7] Like the report, my statement will address CBP's efforts to: (1) Develop schedules and Life-cycle Cost Estimates for the Plan in accordance with best practices, (2) follow key aspects of DHS's acquisition management framework in managing the Plan's three highest-cost programs, and (3) assess the performance of technologies deployed under SBInet and identify mission benefits and develop performance metrics for surveillance technologies to be deployed under the Plan. To conduct work for the March 2014 report, we analyzed DHS and CBP program schedules and Life-cycle Cost Estimates and interviewed DHS and CBP officials responsible for developing and overseeing schedules and cost estimates, including officials from CBP's Office of Technology Innovation and Acquisition (OTIA), which manages implementation of the Plan. We also analyzed DHS and CBP documents, including DHS Acquisition Management Directive 102–01 and its associated DHS Instruction Manual 102–01–001, program briefing slides, budget documents, Acquisition Decision Memorandums, and program risk sheets.[8] Finally, we analyzed performance assessment documentation and metrics used by CBP to determine the effectiveness of technologies deployed under SBInet and interviewed CBP officials responsible for performance measurement activities, and analyzed CBP data on apprehensions, seizures, and asset assists from fiscal year 2010 through June 2013 to determine the extent to which the data could be used to measure the contributions of SBInet technologies in enhancing border security.[9] We conducted this work in accordance with generally accepted Government auditing standards. More detailed information on the scope and methodology of our published report can be found therein.

CBP'S PROGRAM SCHEDULES AND LIFE-CYCLE COST ESTIMATES REFLECT SOME BUT NOT ALL BEST PRACTICES

In our March 2014 report, we assessed OTIA's schedules as of March 2013 for the IFT, RVSS, and MSC programs and found that these program schedules addressed some, but not all, best practices for scheduling. The Schedule Assessment Guide identifies 10 best practices associated with effective scheduling, which are summarized into four characteristics of a reliable schedule—comprehensive, well-constructed, credible, and controlled.[10] According to our overall analysis, OTIA at least

---

[4] The IFT consists of towers with, among other things, ground surveillance radars and surveillance cameras mounted on fixed (that is, stationary) towers. The RVSS includes multiple color and infrared cameras mounted on monopoles, lattice towers, and buildings and differs from the IFT, among other things, in that the RVSS does not include radars. The MSC is a stand-alone, truck-mounted suite of radar and cameras that provides a display within the cab of the truck.

[5] GAO, *Arizona Border Surveillance Technology: More Information on Plans and Costs Is Needed before Proceeding,* GAO–12–22 (Washington, DC: Nov. 4, 2011). A Life-cycle Cost Estimate provides an exhaustive and structured accounting of all resources and associated cost elements required to develop, produce, deploy, and sustain a particular program.

[6] Measures and key attributes are generally defined as part of the business case in order to explain how they contribute to the mission's benefits. See Office of Management and Budget, *OMB Circular No. A–11, Part 7, Section 300, Planning, Budgeting, Acquisition, and Management of Capital Assets* (Washington, DC: Executive Office of the President, July 2010).

[7] GAO–14–368.

[8] DHS Acquisition Management Directive 102–01, Jan. 20, 2010, and DHS Instruction Manual 102–01–001, *Acquisition Management/Instruction Guidebook,* Oct. 1, 2011.

[9] An asset assist is what happens when a technological asset, such as a SBInet surveillance tower, or a non-technological asset, such as a canine team, contributes to apprehensions or seizures. In our March 2014 report, apprehensions data included individuals arrested and identified as deportable aliens, consistent with Border Patrol's definition.

[10] GAO, *GAO Schedule Assessment Guide: Best Practices for Program Schedules,* GAO–12–120G (exposure draft) (Washington, DC: May 2012). We developed this guide through a compilation of best practices that Federal cost-estimating organizations and industry use. According to this guide, for a schedule to be comprehensive, among other things, the schedule should: (1)

Continued

partially met the four characteristics of reliable schedules for the IFT and RVSS schedules (i.e., satisfied about half of the criterion), and partially or minimally met the four characteristics for the MSC schedule, as shown in Table 1. For example, we reported that the schedule for the IFT program partially met the characteristic of being credible in that CBP had performed a schedule risk analysis for the program, but the risk analysis was not based on any connection between risks and specific activities.

TABLE 1.—SUMMARY OF OUR SCHEDULE ASSESSMENTS FOR THE THREE HIGHEST-COST PROGRAMS UNDER THE ARIZONA BORDER SURVEILLANCE TECHNOLOGY PLAN

Schedule Characteristic	Integrated Fixed Towers	Remote Video Surveillance Systems	Mobile Surveillance Capability
Comprehensive	Partially met	Partially met	Partially met
Well constructed	Substantially met	Partially met	Partially met
Credible	Partially met	Partially met	Minimally met
Controlled	Partially met	Partially met	Minimally met

Source.—GAO analysis of Customs and Border Protection data.

Note.—Not met—CBP provided no evidence that satisfies any of the criterion. Minimally met—CBP provided evidence that satisfies a small portion of the criterion. Partially met—CBP provided evidence that satisfies about half of the criterion. Substantially met—CBP provided evidence that satisfies a large portion of the criterion. Met—CBP provided complete evidence that satisfies the entire criterion.

We recommended that CBP ensure that scheduling best practices are applied to the IFT, RVSS, and MSC schedules. DHS concurred with the recommendation and stated that OTIA plans to ensure that scheduling best practices are applied as far as practical when updating the three programs' schedules.

Further, in March 2014 we reported that CBP has not developed an Integrated Master Schedule for the Plan in accordance with best practices. Rather, OTIA has used the separate schedules for each individual program (or "project") to manage implementation of the Plan. OTIA officials stated that an Integrated Master Schedule for the overarching Plan is not needed because the Plan contains individual acquisition programs as opposed to a plan consisting of seven integrated programs. However, collectively these programs are intended to provide CBP with a combination of surveillance capabilities to be used along the Arizona border with Mexico. Moreover, while the programs themselves may be independent of one another, the Plan's resources are being shared among the programs.

OTIA officials stated that when schedules were developed for the Plan's programs, they assumed that personnel would be dedicated to work on individual programs and not be shared between programs. However, as OTIA has initiated and continued work on the Plan's programs, it has shared resources such as personnel among the programs, contributing, in part, to delays experienced by the programs. According to schedule best practices, an Integrated Master Schedule that allows managers to monitor all work activities, how long the activities will take, and how the activities are related to one another is a critical management tool for complex systems that involve the incorporation of a number of different projects, such as the Plan.[11] Thus, we recommended that CBP develop an Integrated Master Schedule for the Plan.

DHS did not concur with this recommendation. In particular, DHS stated that maintaining an Integrated Master Schedule for the Plan undermines the DHS-approved implementation strategy for the individual programs making up the Plan and that a key element of the Plan has been the disaggregation of technology pro-

---

Capture all activities, as defined in the work breakdown structure, (2) reflect what resources are needed to do the work, and (3) establish the duration of all activities and have specific start and end dates. To be well-constructed, among other things, all schedule activities are sequenced in the order that they are to be implemented with the most straightforward logic possible. To be credible, the schedule should reflect the order of events necessary to achieve aggregated products or outcomes, and activities in varying levels of the schedule map to one another. Moreover, a schedule risk analysis should be conducted to predict a level of confidence in meeting the program's completion date. For a schedule to be controlled, the schedule should be updated periodically using actual progress and logic to realistically forecast dates for program activities, and a baseline schedule should be maintained to measure, monitor, and report the program's progress.

[11] GAO–12–120G.

curements. However, we continue to believe that developing an Integrated Master Schedule for the Plan is needed. As we reported in March 2014, this recommendation is not intended to imply that DHS needs to re-aggregate the Plan's seven programs into a "system of systems" or change its procurement strategy in any form. The intent of the recommendation is for DHS to insert the individual schedules for each of the Plan's programs into a single electronic Integrated Master Schedule file in order to identify any resource allocation issues among the programs' schedules. Developing and maintaining an Integrated Master Schedule for the Plan could allow OTIA insight into current or programmed allocation of resources for all programs as opposed to attempting to resolve any resource constraints for each program individually.

In addition in March 2014, we reported that OTIA's rough order of magnitude estimate for the Plan and individual Life-cycle Cost Estimates for the IFT and RVSS programs met some but not all best practices for such estimates. Cost-estimating best practices are summarized into four characteristics—well documented, comprehensive, accurate, and credible.[12] Our analysis of CBP's estimate for the Plan and estimates completed at the time of our review for the IFT and RVSS programs showed that these estimates at least partially met three of these characteristics—well-documented, comprehensive, and accurate. In terms of being credible, these estimates had not been verified with independent cost estimates in accordance with best practices. We recommended that CBP verify the Life-cycle Cost Estimates for the IFT and RVSS programs with independent cost estimates and reconcile any differences.

DHS said it concurred with this recommendation, although we reported that DHS's planned actions will not fully address the intent of the recommendation unless assumptions underlying the cost estimates change. In particular, DHS stated that at this point it does not believe that there would be a benefit in expending funds to obtain independent cost estimates and that if the costs realized to date continue to hold, there may be no requirement or value added in conducting full-blown updates with independent cost estimates. DHS noted, though, that if this assumption changes, OTIA will complete updates and consider preparing independent cost estimates, as appropriate. We recognize the need to balance the cost and time to verify the Life-cycle Cost Estimates with the benefits to be gained from verification with independent cost estimates. However, we continue to believe that independently verifying the Life-cycle Cost Estimates for the IFT and RVSS programs and reconciling any differences, consistent with best practices, could help CBP better ensure the reliability of the estimates.

CBP DID NOT FULLY COMPLETE DOCUMENTS FOR ACQUISITION DECISIONS CONSISTENT WITH THE GUIDANCE

In March 2014, we reported for the Plan's three highest-cost programs—IFT, RVSS, and MSC—DHS and CBP did not consistently approve key acquisition documents before or at the Acquisition Decision Events, in accordance with DHS's acquisition guidance. An important aspect of an Acquisition Decision Event is the review and approval of key acquisition documents critical to establishing the need for a program, its operational requirements, an acquisition baseline, and test and support plans, according to DHS guidance. On the basis of our analysis for IFT, RVSS, and MSC programs under the Plan, we reported that the DHS Acquisition Decision Authority approved the IFT program and the CBP Acquisition Decision Authority approved the RVSS and MSC programs to proceed to subsequent phases in the Acquisition Life-cycle Framework without approving all six required acquisition documents for each program. Furthermore, we reported that one document for the IFT program, five documents for the RVSS program, and two documents for the MSC program were subsequently approved after the programs received authority to proceed to the next phase. DHS plans to complete and approve those documents for the IFT, RVSS, and MSC programs that have not yet been completed and approved.

With regard to one of the required documents—the Test and Evaluation Master Plan—we reported in March 2014 that this document for the IFT program, which was approved by DHS in November 2013, does not describe testing to evaluate the operational effectiveness and suitability of the system. Rather, the Test and Evaluation Master Plan describes CBP's plans to conduct a limited user test of the IFT. According to the Test and Evaluation Master Plan, the limited user test will be de-

---

[12] GAO, *GAO Cost Estimating and Assessment Guide: Best Practices for Developing and Managing Capital Program Costs,* GAO–09–3SP (Washington, DC: March 2009). The methodology outlined in the Cost Estimating and Assessment Guide is a compilation of best practices that Federal cost-estimating organizations and industry use to develop and maintain reliable cost estimates throughout the life of an acquisition program.

signed to determine the IFT's mission contribution. According to OTIA and the Test and Evaluation Master Plan, this testing is planned to occur during 30 days in environmental conditions present at one site—the Nogales station. CBP plans to conduct limited user testing for the IFT under the same process that is typically performed in any operational test and evaluation, according to the Test and Evaluation Master Plan. The November 2013 IFT Test and Evaluation Master Plan notes that, because the IFT acquisition strategy is to acquire non-developmental IFT systems from the marketplace (sometimes referred to as a commercial off-the-shelf system), a limited user test will provide Border Patrol with the information it needs to determine the mission contributions from the IFTs, and thus CBP does not plan to conduct more robust testing. However, this approach is not consistent with DHS's acquisition guidance, which states that even for commercial off-the-shelf systems, operational test and evaluation should occur in the environmental conditions in which a system will be used before a full production decision for the system is made and the system is subsequently deployed.

As we reported, we recognize the need to balance the cost and time to conduct testing to determine the IFT's operational effectiveness and suitability with the benefits to be gained from such testing. Although the limited user test should help provide CBP with information on the IFTs' mission contribution and how Border Patrol can use the system in its operations, the limited user test does not position CBP to obtain information on how the IFTs may perform under the various environmental conditions the system could face once deployed. Conducting limited user testing in one area in Arizona—the Nogales station—for 30 days could limit the information available to CBP on how the IFT may perform in other conditions and locations along the Arizona border with Mexico. As of November 2013, CBP intended to deploy IFTs to 50 locations in southern Arizona, which can include differences in terrain and climate throughout the year.

We recommended that CBP revise the IFT Test and Evaluation Master Plan to more fully test the IFT program, before beginning full production, in the various environmental conditions in which IFTs will be used to determine operational effectiveness and suitability. DHS did not concur with this recommendation and stated that the Test and Evaluation Master Plan includes tailored testing and user assessments that will provide much, if not all, of the insight contemplated by the intent of the recommendation. However, as we reported in March 2014, we continue to believe that revising the Test and Evaluation Master Plan to include more robust testing to determine operational effectiveness and suitability could better position CBP to evaluate IFT capabilities before moving to full production for the system, help provide CBP with information on the extent to which the towers satisfy Border Patrol's user requirements, and help reduce potential program risks.

CBP HAS IDENTIFIED MISSION BENEFITS, BUT DOES NOT CAPTURE COMPLETE DATA ON THE CONTRIBUTIONS OF ITS SURVEILLANCE TECHNOLOGIES

We reported in March 2014 that CBP has identified the mission benefits of its surveillance technologies, but does not capture complete data on the contributions of these technologies, which in combination with other relevant performance metrics or indicators, could be used to better determine the contributions of CBP's surveillance technologies and inform resource allocation decisions. CBP has identified mission benefits of surveillance technologies to be deployed under the Plan, such as improved situational awareness and agent safety.

While CBP has defined these mission benefits, the agency has not developed key attributes for performance metrics for all surveillance technologies to be deployed as part of the Plan, as we recommended in November 2011.[13] In our April 2013 update on the progress made by the agencies to address our findings on duplication and cost savings across the Federal Government, CBP officials stated that operations of its two SBInet surveillance systems identified examples of key attributes for metrics that can be useful in assessing the Plan's implementation for technologies.[14] For example, according to CBP officials, to help measure whether illegal activity has decreased, examples of key attributes include decreases in the amount of arrests, complaints by ranchers and other citizens, and destruction of public and private lands and property. While the development of key attributes for metrics for the two SBInet surveillance systems is a positive step, CBP has not identified attributes for metrics for all technologies to be acquired and deployed as part of the Plan. Thus, to fully address the intent of our recommendation, CBP would need to

---

[13] GAO–12–22.

[14] GAO, *2013 Annual Report: Actions Needed to Reduce Fragmentation, Overlap, and Duplication and Achieve Other Financial Benefits,* GAO–13–279SP, (Washington, DC: Apr. 9, 2013).

develop and apply key attributes for performance metrics for each of the technologies to be deployed under the Plan to assess its progress in implementing the Plan and determine when mission benefits have been fully realized.

Furthermore, we reported in March 2014 that CBP is not capturing complete asset assist data on the contributions of its surveillance technologies to apprehensions and seizures, and these data are not being consistently recorded by Border Patrol agents and across locations. Although CBP has a field within its Enforcement Integrated Database (EID) for maintaining data on whether technological assets, such as SBInet surveillance towers, and non-technological assets, such as canine teams, assisted or contributed to the apprehension of illegal entrants, and seizure of drugs and other contraband, according to CBP officials, Border Patrol agents are not required to record these data.[15] This limits CBP's ability to collect, track, and analyze available data on asset assists to help monitor the contribution of surveillance technologies, including its SBInet system, to Border Patrol apprehensions and seizures and inform resource allocation decisions.

We reported that according to our analysis of EID asset assist data for apprehensions and seizures in the Tucson and Yuma sectors from fiscal year 2010 through June 2013, information on asset assists was generally not recorded for all apprehension and seizure events.[16] For instance, for the 166,976 apprehension events reported by the Border Patrol across the Tucson sector during fiscal year 2010 through June 2013, an asset assist was not recorded for 115,517 (or about 69 percent) of these apprehension events. In the Yuma sector, of the 8,237 apprehension events reported by Border Patrol agents during the specified time period, an asset assist was not recorded for 7,150 (or about 87 percent) of these apprehension events. Since data on asset assists are not required to be reported, it is unclear whether the data were not reported because an asset was not a contributing factor in the apprehension or seizure or whether an asset was a contributing factor but was not recorded by agents.

As a result, CBP is not positioned to determine the contribution of surveillance technologies in the apprehension of illegal entrants and seizure of drugs and other contraband during the specified time frame. We reported that an associate chief at Border Patrol told us that while data on asset assists are not systematically recorded and tracked, Border Patrol recognizes the benefits of assessments of asset assists data, including those from surveillance technologies, such as the SBInet system. The associate chief further noted that these data in combination with other data, such as numbers of apprehensions and seizures, are used on a limited basis to help the agency make adjustments to its acquisition plans prior to deploying resources, thereby enabling the agency to make more informed deployment decisions.

We recommended that CBP require data on asset assists to be recorded and tracked within EID and that once these data are required to recorded and tracked, analyze available data on apprehensions and technological assists, in combination with other relevant performance metrics or indicators, as appropriate, to determine the contribution of surveillance technologies to CBP's border security efforts. CBP concurred with our recommendations and stated that Border Patrol is changing its data collection process to allow for improved reporting on asset assists for apprehensions and seizures and intends to make it mandatory to record whether an asset assisted in an apprehension or seizure. DHS plans to change its process by December 31, 2014.

Chairwoman Miller, Ranking Member Jackson Lee, and Members of the subcommittee, this concludes my prepared statement. I would be pleased to answer any questions that you may have.

Mrs. MILLER. Thank you very much.

I think, Mr. Borkowski, I will pick up right where Ms. Gambler on her last point there about this asset assist.

I am not quite sure the mechanics of how that would work, but I suppose that is something out in the field where as they would—

---

[15] In addition to maintaining data on asset assists, the Border Patrol collects and maintains data on apprehensions and seizures in DHS's EID.

[16] In our March 2014 report, we defined an "apprehension or seizure event" as the occasion on which Border Patrol agents make an apprehension of an illegal entrant or a seizure of drugs or other contraband. The event is recorded in the EID and a date and unique identifying number are assigned. An event can involve the apprehension of one or multiple illegal entrants or types of items, and each individual illegal entrant apprehended or type of item seized in the event is associated with the assigned unique identifying number. Our analysis of apprehension events included instances in which an event had at least one deportable individual.

as they are going through their checklist of how an apprehension happened or whatever the incident was.

What is your thought about why you are not accumulating that kind of information? Is it just too much of a burden for the folks out in the field or you don't think it would be worth its time or what?

Mr. BORKOWSKI. I think the issue at this point is just having the systems and the capacity to do that. We generally have the information. The question is how do we get that recorded and documented, but the Border Patrol is working on that and it is committed to doing that because we believe it does tell us something.

I would caution about how much it tells us, right, because you get in situations where various components came together to produce an apprehension and it is tempting to say this apprehension was caused by the agent or this apprehension was caused by the technology.

Ultimately, we like to get that sensitivity—how much can we attribute to technology, but the reality is these things merge together. So I think we want to collect the data, but I would caution until we collect it and study it, it is still an open question as to how much utility that will provide us downstream in terms of a reasonable performance metric.

Mrs. MILLER. You know I asked that question because as you are aware, this subcommittee unanimously and the full committee unanimously passed our border bill which is going to be an accountability matrix at the border in utilizing various kinds of systems and whatever we can to really be able to effectively have accountability and measure our success or failure for that matter, so that won't be the end of that line of questioning I would guess.

I also wanted to pick up on something you mentioned about a 75 percent savings. As you said, to paraphrase, it is something that doesn't normally happen in Government to have a 75 percent savings, and I guess I would ask both of you this question of whether or not Ms. Gambler was surprised to see the 75 percent savings, and what was the construct of that budget request to have a 75 percent savings.

I know that the Department of Homeland Security would have had to review your budget request. Did they have all the pieces available? It certainly calls in to—makes us think a bit about some of the budget requests that we are seeing.

Mr. BORKOWSKI. I think what is important to understand is first of all where those numbers come from. Life-cycle cost estimate, right. That was a term you heard. In life-cycle cost estimates there are a bunch of methodologies of generating them, but they are all based on experience.

When it comes right down to it, you get a life-cycle cost estimate based on your past experiences and you try to find the closest examples of systems like the things you are buying and what did they cost.

But when your experience is all based on that, "I am not going to the lot to buy a car. Instead I am going to go find somebody; I am going to ask them to build me a car from scratch." That is where most of our cost experience is from, so that is what comes into a life-cycle cost estimate.

The GAO looks at this. We look at this. Did they follow best practices? The answer is largely I would argue it did based on the way we do life-cycle cost estimates.

But we tried to buy these differently. We tried to buy them by going to the lot. You can imagine the difference it would cost me to get a car if I went to Sam's manufacturing plant and said build me a car from scratch or if I go to the local Ford or Chrysler or GM dealer, whoever I go to.

I think in your own mind you can imagine the difference between those, so that is factor No. 1. By the way, I was surprised by 75 percent. When we built the life-cycle cost estimate, and I think if we go back to testimony of this committee and similar discussions, there was some concern; is that number too low?

We were arguing we put contingency in it because we are doing something that we haven't done before, but I was surprised by 75 percent to be honest. I was hopeful we would have cost savings. I was actually surprised by 75 percent.

Here is the other thing that happens, and I have been trying to find a good way to make this case because these are subtle things that are hugely important as it turns out.

A lot of times when we want performance in something—let's say I want 90 percent probability detection. When I am designing that from scratch because of the way we test it, I actually have to design it to say 93, 94, 95 percent even though what I want is 90 percent.

The reason is the statistics that go into testing to be sure that I really get 90. So I am trying to think of an analogy here, and I am in your area, not mine, but this is what it looks like to me.

You are running a campaign for election and you have got two candidates. You need 50 percent of the vote and you run a poll. The poll says I have 51 percent.

Now you may feel comfortable about that but in the fine print it says with a margin of certainty plus or minus 3 percent, which means the poll really said you have somewhere between 48 and 54, so now you have a decision I would think. Do you go after that last 3 percent to make sure you don't hit the 48?

That costs a lot more than the first 3 percent cost. That is exactly what happens to us when we buy things. Going from 90 to 95 percent to guarantee I got 90 percent—that costs a lot more than the first 5 percent did.

When I go and buy the things off the lot and I say look tell me what you have got and we will accept your definition of it because I don't really care about 1 or 2 percent either way, huge cost savings. So it looks like that is what happened here.

I think that this is something new, and that is another point I think when we do something new we have to tailor the past practices to the thing that is new.

I believe we need to study this some more. I believe the jury is still out, but it looks to me like a good deal of this is real.

Mrs. MILLER. I am going to ask Ms. Gambler to respond as well, but in regards to your analogies being from the motor city, I would stay away from the campaign analogies. Stick with the car analogies. They are better.

[Laughter.]

Mrs. MILLER. Ms. Gambler.

Ms. GAMBLER. I would just add that I think that what will be important going forward and in looking at the contract and the deployment of these IFT's is how CBP, how the Government will hold the contractor accountable and provide that oversight for the systems that are being deployed.

From our perspective what isn't clear from the test plans that we have seen from CBP thus far is how they will be able to ensure that the IFTs once deployed are meeting the Border Patrol's operational needs and will work and the locations and under the conditions that those technologies planned to be deployed.

So I think what is critical here going forward is how CBP will be positioned to have the information it needs to provide oversight for the contractor in the systems that are being deployed.

Mrs. MILLER. Just one other question and for both of you as well and this would be in regards to the testing that has been done which the GAO mentioned is one of the recommendations, and you had some concerns about all of that.

We just want to make sure it is working, right? When we think about the lessons learned and the involvement or not enough involvement perhaps of those that are—the customers really—the end-users of this is the folks in the field.

Could you expand a little bit on the testing that was done and why you feel that this is going to work and why you are—why GAO is raising this as a concern about the amount of testing that was done and how it all unfolded?

Mr. BORKOWSKI. First of all, what was done was a demo. Remember, we wanted something that was on the lot so we wanted bidders to prove to us that it was really on the lot and it wasn't just a brochure.

So the bidders actually had to take their system out to the field, take it out of the box, turn it on, and show that it did what they said it would do, which is unique. We don't normally do that.

By the way, most of industry asked us to do that because they said, you know, Fred is going to lie to you but I am telling the truth, but you won't know it unless you make both of us prove it.

So it was a demo. It was not a full-blown test. However, these are systems that have been around for a while and we were able to get an initial indication of that.

The other thing that I want to emphasize is, it is not like there will be no testing. There will. There is a term of art that is being tossed around here called operational test and evaluation, but there is a whole bunch of different kinds of test and evaluation, so we will have extensive testing that these systems produce the results that were committed to in the contract.

That will start with something called system acceptance test, which technically is developmental test and evaluation, so there is a whole rubric here that comes into play.

Then limited user testing is a test that is operational test and evaluation designed to meet the Border Patrol's desire to get answers to its questions.

So what we have actually done, rather than formal operational test and evaluation is sat down with the Border Patrol and said, what do you want to check out? What do you want to know about the system?

That is all documented. It is all committed. All of that testing will be done to advise the Border Patrol on how much more of this it wants to do.

So we are doing the intent of that, but when I go to formal operational test and evaluation I create aspirational goals that get me to that 3 percent more problem that I was describing and that is what we want to avoid.

So we have tailored the approach to this, but there is extensive testing intended in this plan.

Mrs. MILLER. Ms. Gambler.

Ms. GAMBLER. I think what is key here is that testing helps an agency manage risks and it doesn't necessarily mean that there is going to be fewer problems. It just means you are getting information on potential risks or potential risks of problems to a system earlier on in the process than you might otherwise have.

That information is key to providing program managers with what they need to know and what they need to do to address any issues that comes up, and then positions them to be able to address those issues earlier in the process.

So from our perspective there is an opportunity here for CBP to do more robust testing than what they currently plan to do to help ensure that the technology that is delivered by the vendor meets Border Patrol's needs and will operate in the different environments where the towers are intended to be placed.

We think this is important given—or in light of some of the testing challenges that SBInet encountered including, for example, the Army Test and Evaluation Command identifying that there were some issues with how terrain affected the radars of SBInet. The ATEC officials referred to it as a technology terrain mismatch.

So we think in light of those challenges there is an opportunity here for CBP to do some additional testing that would give them the information they need to effectively manage the program.

Mrs. MILLER. Thank you very much.

The Chairwoman recognizes the gentlelady from Texas.

Ms. JACKSON LEE. Ms. Gambler, if I might pose a question to you. Based on your work on the Arizona Border Surveillance Technology Plan and GAO's prior work on SBInet are there similar challenges of warning signs you are seeing with the plan that GAO believed contributed to some of SBInet's failures? What must be done to address these warning signs?

Ms. GAMBLER. Based on our work, DHS and CBP certainly have followed best practices and DHS' acquisition guidance in certain areas, but we did report that they faced similar types of challenges in managing the plan as they encountered under SBInet.

For example, for both SBInet and the new Arizona technology plan we identified that CBP has schedules and life-cycle cost estimates that don't substantially meet best practices in all areas.

As I mentioned, for both SBInet and the Arizona technology plan, we identified some challenges with test plans for those two systems and for both SBInet and the Arizona technology plan we identified in both cases that CBP hadn't identified performance metrics for assessing basically what we are getting for the technology. So in those areas there are similar types of challenges between the two systems.

What we have done is made recommendations to DHS and CBP both on SBInet and the new Arizona technology plan to get at some of those challenges to make sure that they more fully adopt and use best practices for scheduling and life-cycle cost estimating and also that they establish metrics for assessing the contributions of technologies to border security and that they collect data to be able to assess those metrics.

Ms. JACKSON LEE. Do you have an update? Have they begun to do that specifically with life cycles and the test plan? Do you have a report that says where they are now?

Ms. GAMBLER. So the recommendations we made with regard to SBInet have largely been closed because SBInet has been canceled. In terms of the recommendations that we have made as it relates to the Arizona technology plan, we made those——

Ms. JACKSON LEE. I know that SBI has been—I am speaking about going forward. The new proposal.

Ms. GAMBLER. Sure. We made those recommendations in the report being released today and CBP does plan to take some actions in response to that.

For example, the Border Patrol is starting to work to make changes to how it collects data on asset assists so that it can set some metrics for how to assess contributions of border surveillance technologies and CBP also has plans to look at their schedules and life-cycle cost estimates as well.

As they are updating those, they have plans to make sure that they do more fully comply with best practices.

Ms. JACKSON LEE. How do you know that?

Ms. GAMBLER. That is what they reported to us in terms of what they plan to do, Ranking Member Jackson Lee, and we will continue to monitor their progress in response to those recommendations as they start to implement those actions.

Ms. JACKSON LEE. How long would they need for compliance? How long would they need to engage in the process?

Ms. GAMBLER. For the different recommendations they have set different time frames for completion. Some of them are 6 months to a year out and we will, as I said, continue to monitor their progress and would be happy to update you on their progress as they go forward.

Ms. JACKSON LEE. So as we stand now from the recommendations made by GAO, CBP is not in compliance? Going forward, not on SBInet, which I know has been canceled.

Ms. GAMBLER. Correct. CBP right now has not yet implemented the recommendations we have made.

Ms. JACKSON LEE. What is the give-and-take to—again I am going back—what is the give-and-take to expect compliance? What is the engagement and the report back that you get?

Ms. GAMBLER. For recommendations that we make on any report, we regularly follow up with the agency to determine the status of actions they are taking in response to the recommendations.

That could be exchange of documents or meetings with agency officials and then we make an assessment of the extent to which the actions that the agency has taken are responsive to the intent of our recommendation.

Ms. JACKSON LEE. When do you expect then to get back with CBP on these present recommendations?

Ms. GAMBLER. Some of the recommendations they indicated about 6 months or so, that we might be able to start getting some information from them, so that would probably be the time frame that we will start to follow up.

Ms. JACKSON LEE. Mr. Borkowski, you acknowledge SBInet and in my statement I acknowledged that it was $1 billion in cost. You have now engaged with Elbit Systems of America on the deployment of integrated fixed towers and that valued contract was $145 million although the initial projected cost was $600 million.

To what do you attribute the significant cost discrepancy? Do we have a quality product? You just heard GAO, Ms. Gambler, mention that you are not yet in compliance. You have indicated at least 6 months on certain aspects of the testing aspect.

So would you comment on again the cost discrepancy? Is this a lesser technology than originally planned? Do you think you will see more inaccuracies? Are you confident that we have got the best contractor, but more importantly, is this a true answer to SBInet?

Mr. BORKOWSKI. With the last question, we are not trying to—in terms of the correction of the errors that led to SBInet, I think it is a good chunk of the way, 80, 90 percent of the way there. I do think that.

Is this a good contractor? The system—we had many bidders, many bidders, and of those many bidders we saw several systems that appear to work right out of the box.

The one that we awarded is actually used for border security in Israel as it turns out, but there were other bidders who had very effective systems of that worked right out of the box, so that is something different.

Our sense is that the quality is high, and I think the cost difference is due to what I tried to describe earlier. When we buy things and go to a specialty shop to build them from scratch we pay more than when we buy something off the lot.

Now if there is nothing off the lot to buy then we are stuck with going to a specialty vendor and that is the way we bought SBInet. The problem was there was stuff on the lot, so when we changed to that you have a significant impact.

Then when I go to those folks and say look, I am not asking you. I am going to tell you what I am interested in, but I am not asking you to go to the last 3 percent. Tell me what you can do, give me some reason to believe that, and if that is good enough for me I will buy it.

It is that last 3 percent cost that cost you an arm and a leg, so I think those are all things that led to this significant cost reduction. By the way, that $145 million covers 50 towers in Arizona and 7 years of operations and maintenance, so it is quite a bit of functionality that we get out of it.

What we saw in the demos was very impressive. I don't know if the Border Patrol would say this, but when they described what they saw in that system in the demo, they almost were raving about it to be frank. Hopefully that will get us to where we want——

Ms. JACKSON LEE. Thank you.

Let me ask if I might, will you wrap this into the question that I am going to give you? I just want to make sure you answer, Ms. Gambler, that you will be making a definitive effort to follow through on the life cycle and test plan testing.

But my question that I want to ask is in my statement I mentioned the Border Patrol Chief Michael Fisher informed the office that the Border Patrol needs fewer integrated fixed towers in Arizona than originally planned and instead wants more mobile surveillance technology to be used in South Texas—more mobile surveillance technology to be used which has increasingly become a hot spot for illicit cross-border activity in recent years meaning more of that in South Texas.

Given that it has been 3 years since the cancellation of SBInet, keeping in mind the dynamic situation along the border, how confident are you that the number and type of technologies planned for the Arizona border is appropriate? How do you plan to address Chief Fisher's inquiries, if you would?

Thank you, Madam Chairwoman.

Mr. BORKOWSKI. Certainly. Chief Fisher has maintained the requirement for all of the IFTs but he has said they are lower priority, so there is a subtle distinction there, but he says that is still a requirement.

However, he would like to divert resources and do things in South Texas first. So what we have done there is, as you know, we have for example put up and these are demonstrations and evaluations, they are kind of temporary activities, but we have flown some aero stats there.

The one part of the Arizona technology plan is a system called the mobile video surveillance system also known as a scope truck. It has got an infrared camera that is long-range that sees. The Border Patrol asked us to divert those to South Texas. That contract will be awarded around June.

In addition, the contract that awarded it mobile surveillance capabilities, those are going to Arizona and will free up resources that will then be moved to South Texas; mobile resources that will be moved to South Texas.

The other element of this is that again, as I have said we have saved some cost and the Border Patrol has asked us to prioritize those costs savings not in filling in the IFT in Arizona just yet, but in applying those resources to continue the kinds of things we have been doing in moving mobile video surveillance systems using DOD technology in South Texas. So to this point that is what we are able to do relatively quickly.

Ms. JACKSON LEE. Thank you. I look forward to this continuing dialogue. I think it is going to be crucial as this system is put in place. I hope there is some synergism between GAO and DHS in getting this right. Thank you.

I yield back, Madam Chairwoman.

Mrs. MILLER. The Chairwoman now recognizes the gentleman from South Carolina, Mr. Duncan.

Mr. DUNCAN. Thank you, Madam Chairwoman.

Just to remind the committee, we are well over $17 trillion in debt. That is how big our financial hole is as a Nation. Hearing after hearing before the Oversight Management and Efficiency Subcommittee which I chair, we have identified DHS programs that have overspent and failed to fully deliver.

Having been down there to the border in Arizona I know first-hand how rugged the terrain is. I was surprised to see that CBP plans only to test the towers in one location for 1 month, and I question how much sense that makes.

Mr. Borkowski, I get the need to get these towers deployed. Listen, I appreciate technology being used, and I like the idea of integrated towers. I like the idea of aero stats. I like the idea of more different surveillance that can aid the CBP officers on the ground.

We have got to have a multi-pronged approach. That includes fencing, that includes personnel, and that includes surveillance, so I get that. I get the need to deploy these quickly, but we have been down this road before of inadequate testing with SBInet. So what makes you think that you are in the best position for success with only one test?

Mr. BORKOWSKI. Again, I think it is a misnomer to say there will be only one test. There will be extensive tests and the plan as it is written says we will test for as long as the Border Patrol wants to test.

In fact, the appropriations act that was passed has language that we supported and already intended to do which says we will not do subsequent deployments until the chief of the Border Patrol says he is comfortable doing subsequent deployments.

Mr. DUNCAN. Let me ask you this. This is pretty expensive technology. This contract is a fairly substantial reward. How much testing, real testing have been done by the contractor at no cost to the Government because we have got to be good stewards and if they want the contract they have got to—in the private sector, if somebody wants a contract, they get out there, they do all the testing, and they prove to the purchaser of their equipment that they have done the testing, so how much of that has gone on to save the taxpayers?

Mr. BORKOWSKI. Well, we did run, as I said, demonstrations. We did make them take their system and put it up out along the Southwest Border, turn it on, and show us how it worked for a couple of days, but remember——

Mr. DUNCAN. For a couple of days.

Mr. BORKOWSKI. Well, but they also, remember, they have deployed these in Israel. They have been using them for a significant amount of time.

There is another element to testing that I think is getting lost in the discussion here, and it goes to this idea of a system development versus an off-the-shelf system.

A lot of this discussion about testing incrementally comes when you say okay, I am going to build—let's go to the car example. If I were going and building a car from scratch and designing it from scratch and went to Joe's manufacturing company, when Joe built the carburetor, I would test the carburetor.

When Joe built the engine, I would test the engine. I would test all of the sub pieces, and then I start to put subcomponents together and test, and then I put the whole thing together and test. That is the kind of testing you do as you go.

But when you have a whole car already built and you bought it off the lot, you don't tear it apart to test the carburetor and the engine. You test the whole car, and you test it once you have bought it.

That is exactly what we are doing. It is a change in paradigm because we are not doing system development, but we are doing testing.

So I don't think we are all getting the accurate picture here. That testing as I say we have designed with the Border Patrol to say we will test everything you want to test to answer your questions, and we will not do another thing until you tell us you are comfortable but I still have to buy the car. I went and bought it off the lot. I do have to buy the car so I can test it and that is what we are doing.

Mr. DUNCAN. I appreciate that. Let me shift gears here for just a minute. The GAO's report raises questions as to whether acquisition management lessons learned from SBInet are being applied to the new technology plan.

I understand that there is some disagreement and that CBP has not concurred with all of the recommendations of the most recent report, so why did the Department not concur on two of GAO's suggested recommendations?

Mr. BORKOWSKI. Basically, because in our view, those two recommendations drive us back to system development, back to that approach that says I am not going to buy the car off the lot, I am going to go to Joe's manufacturing company and build one from scratch.

Plus, the other thing that they do is they take us back to the days of SBInet where we had everything all tied together as one program and couldn't pull the pieces apart.

So the one recommendation we non-concurred on was for something called an IMS, an integrated master schedule, which again is a sort of a term of art. It is a schedule but it is a schedule on steroids.

It has got all kinds of interconnections and networking at very low levels of detail and each program has an integrated master schedule, and we did that on purpose. We want separate programs. I want to be able to buy IFT whether or not I buy RVSS and so forth and so on.

The GAO says that we should take all of those separate programs and create an IMS for them as one program. That is not consistent with DHS practice and what it has the effect of doing is turning us back into SBInet. We think that is a really bad idea.

The second recommendation that we non-concurred with had to do with operational test and evaluation. Not in the spirit, because as I have already explained, we are going to do all of those things with the Border Patrol, but when you do formal operational test and evaluation you set targets.

As I was explaining to the Chairwoman, if I set a target of 90 percent I actually have to pay to get to 95 percent to prove I can do 90 percent. We do not want to do that. We do not want to pay that premium. We do not need to pay that premium, so in our view, those two recommendations are driving us exactly back to the things we tried not to do after we got out from under SBInet.

Mr. DUNCAN. I am following acquisition very closely, so I am interested to see how this actually transpires.

I don't want to sit here, Madam Chairwoman, 2 years from now and try to justify to the American taxpayer why we had another SBInet and wasted their money. I hope this works.

I am interested in seeing it, and I am going to wish for the success because security at the Southwest Border is very important to folks in South Carolina and across this Nation.

I have got some other comments and questions. I will just wait.

Ms. Gambler, I want you to chime in so I am going to wait for the second round hopefully and with that, I will just yield back.

Ms. JACKSON LEE. Could I just ask you to yield just for one moment?

I just want to thank you for the work you have done on contracts or procurement. I have said it on some of the hearings. I just want this one sentence. We all want this to work. We are in a new world and again I just want to repeat that our critique today is to make it better for America.

I yield back.

Mr. DUNCAN. Thanks to the lady and the critique will make it better. I think that is what the Chairwoman is wanting on this to make sure that, (A) acquisition is happening. We are not spending taxpayer dollars recklessly and that we are making good decisions for the Nation. We are applying best management practices and we will secure the border and stop the flow of illegals into the country.

With that, I yield back.

Mrs. MILLER. Absolutely.

The Chairwoman now recognizes the gentleman from Texas, Mr. O'Rourke.

Mr. O'ROURKE. Thank you, Madam Chairwoman.

For Mr. Borkowski, how much will we spend on the Arizona Border Surveillance Technology Plan?

Mr. BORKOWSKI. I am trying to add up the pieces in my head here. Our original estimates back when we first advertised the planned——

Mr. O'ROURKE. I just want to know what we are going to spend.

Mr. BORKOWSKI. I am thinking it will be $500 million to $700 million for deployment plus up to 10 years of operation and maintenance. I am thinking it will be in that ballpark when it is all said and done.

Mr. O'ROURKE. Five hundred million dollars to $700 million for deployment and what is O&M cost over 10 years?

Mr. BORKOWSKI. It is included in that number, so I would expect it would be roughly 50-50 between the deployment cost and the O&M cost for 10 years. That is a ballpark figure.

Mr. O'ROURKE. Okay. Going back to SBInet which I understand you were the executive director of before moving to this current position, we spent $1 billion and have a 53 miles monitored, so roughly just under $19 million a mile.

In learning from SBInet and looking forward to what we are doing here with the Arizona Border Surveillance Technology Plan, one of the pieces that was missing before I think were performance metrics that we would be able to look at and know whether or not we had a success.

What are the performance metrics for this?

Mr. BORKOWSKI. The performance metrics for this are basically to—and we tailored them—to ask technology to look in areas where technology can see.

So you heard for example that we couldn't see through rough terrain——

Mr. O'ROURKE. I want to know to answer my colleague from South Carolina's question, in 2 years, in 5 years, in 10 years, when we are looking back at the $600 million plus that we have spent, how do we know that it was a success?

What are the objective numbers that I am going to be able to look at to make an objective judgment on whether or not that was money well-spent?

Mr. BORKOWSKI. When you combine this technology with effectiveness ratio, I think you will get the numbers you are looking for. So what we will be able to tell you is, is or is not something going on, how much activity is in that area, and then the Border Patrol will be able to tell you of that activity how much did they interdict. I believe that is what you are looking for.

Mr. O'ROURKE. Okay. I don't know that I totally understand that. I would hope that when we are going to spend this kind of money on the heels of I think one of the worst, most missed managed Federal projects in SBInet, a billion-dollar boondoggle that didn't work and netted us 53 miles, I am not sure how we are doing in those 53 miles.

When the GAO assesses that, makes recommendations, and you choose not to implement those recommendations when you don't have clear performance metrics, when you don't have an integrated master schedule, when you don't have the true life-cycle cost estimates, when you say something like tell me what you can do and I will buy it to a vendor when I think we had vendors really controlling the situation in SBInet and kind of designing it as they went along.

When you say that you are flexible on the technical details but you don't have a coherent way to measure what we are going to do, I am worried that we are going to have something akin to SBInet again.

To again answer the concerns from my colleague from South Carolina I watched a couple of years ago as a private citizen in an El Paso border community the god-awful waste that was SBInet and I swore that I would never allow something like that to happen again.

So I don't want to hope that we are not going to have this problem again. I want to stop it in its tracks now before we get there. If we had not had the problem with SBInet, I think some of what we are talking about today might be forgivable or understandable, but following that why not follow the recommendations of the GAO?

I think it is—frankly it is a very difficult to hear you say that the GAO is trying to point you in the direction of replicating the errors of SBInet basically blaming the GAO for sending you back into SBInet when I think it was the GAO that uncovered the awful problems within SBInet.

I really—I have just got to say for the record, Madam Chairwoman, I think we need to stop this program now until you can adequately describe what the performance metrics are, what the value is that we are going to get for this money that is adding to the National debt and a better answer as to why you are not going to comply with the recommendations from the GAO.

I find today's testimony just very troubling for all of the reasons we have talked about from border security to the value of taxpayer dollars to official oversight and accountability from CBP.

I think this money could be much better used in much better ways.

With that, Madam Chairwoman, I will conclude.

Mrs. MILLER. I thank the gentleman for his statement and his concerns.

Neither myself or the Ranking Member have any additional questions.

Does the gentleman from South Carolina wish to ask—take some additional time?

Mr. DUNCAN. Thank you.

I would just like for Ms. Gambler to chime in on the last question I asked about the Department not concurring with GAO's suggested recommendations and the differences between what GAO has said and what maybe Mr. Borkowski testified to.

Ms. GAMBLER. Thank you, Congressman Duncan.

From our perspective our findings and our recommendations are not intending for DHS or CBP to create a system of systems or re-aggregate programs under the Arizona technology plan.

Rather, they are intended to help ensure that CBP consistently follows best practices and acquisition guidance and those best practices and acquisition guidance exist and are designed to help ensure that acquisitions are managed effectively and efficiently and that acquisition programs deliver to meet operational needs.

So for example, with regard to the integrated master schedule recommendation that we made—again, our intent isn't for CBP to re-aggregate programs under that schedule.

The intent of our recommendation is that DHS or CBP would take the schedules that they have for the individual programs, insert them into one master schedule file, and by doing that CBP could look at resource constraints or resource issues across the different programs and resolve those issues as they come up rather than resolving them on a program-by-program individual basis.

Mr. DUNCAN. I apologize for interrupting you. They don't have a master schedule now for the complete program to my understanding. Is that correct?

Ms. GAMBLER. That is what our finding is, yes.

We would also added that an integrated master schedule is viewed as being a good practice because even where there aren't direct linkages between programs, in cases where programs are being reported to a single customer or single client, in this case the Border Patrol, it is helpful to have the schedules inserted into one file so that for reporting purposes the customer or client can have a comprehensive or a concise view of the programs and understand when the programs will be completed and when the overall plan will be completed.

Mr. DUNCAN. Thank you.

I really don't have anything further, Madam Chairwoman. I just wanted to give Ms. Gambler a chance to chime in and I ran out of time.

Thank you so much for going back.

Mrs. MILLER. You are welcome.

Ms. JACKSON LEE. Madam Chairwoman, I don't have a question either. I just want to say this as I keep hearing integrated systems let me be very clear. Coming from Texas and being engaged in the border for all of these years, I want to see the strategic approach that is in a bill that has not yet passed the floor of the House, but a very good bill.

I want to hear about California, Texas, New Mexico, Arizona, and as we are discussing this, this is the title of this hearing—dealing with the Arizona fixed issues, I want to make sure that we are consistently saying to DHS, we want a consistent, responsible, respected border approach to allow for the free flow of those who come to do us good and who want to come and do many things that have added to our economy but also to be able to be in a block for those who want to do us harm.

But we want to hear about Texas and Arizona, New Mexico, and California collectively together as it relates to the Southern Border and of course I always make mention of the Chairwoman's very important area, the Northern Border.

I yield back, Madam Chairwoman.

Mrs. MILLER. I thank all of the—certainly thank the witnesses today, and I thank my colleagues for that which I think is a very informative hearing. As it was just mentioned by the Ranking Member, we actually have, as you know Mr. Borkowski, SBInet that was deployed on the Northern Border and a section actually in my district and we have had pretty good success with it.

It may be the one area of SBInet that people point to as it has been quite helpful in that particular area, but also as has been mentioned here we have this border bill that we hope to see some movement on in the House and one of the biggest components of that and I think has been a lot of debate across the country is how the Senate bill in our mind treats border security as just throwing huge pots of money at the border again in an ad hoc fashion without really having these accountability matrixes, et cetera and something that we all discussed during the construct of that bill was SBInet and the amount of money that we spent there and the failures that we have had there, et cetera.

So I think as you can see clearly from this subcommittee and I think we can say as well the full committee we are really going to be watching this thing. We are really going to be looking at it, so there remains a number of questions.

At this time I would say to the Members of the committee if they have any additional questions for the witnesses, we would ask you witnesses then to respond in writing.

Pursuant to Committee Rule 7(e), the hearing record will be held open for 10 days, and without objection, the committee stands adjourned. Thank you.

[Whereupon, at 11:07 a.m., the subcommittee was adjourned.]

○